The Life of a TURTLE

Clare Hibbert

www.raintreepublishers.co.uk
Visit our website to find out more information about **Raintree** books.

To order:
 Phone 44 (0) 1865 888112
Send a fax to 44 (0) 1865 314091
Visit the Raintree Bookshop at **www.raintreepublishers.co.uk** to browse our catalogue and order online.

First published in Great Britain by Raintree, Halley Court, Jordan Hill, Oxford OX2 8EJ, part of Harcourt Education.
Raintree is a registered trademark of Harcourt Education Ltd.

Editorial: Nick Hunter and Catherine Clarke
Design: Michelle Lisseter and Tipani Design (www.tipani.co.uk)
Illustration: Tony Jones, Art Construction
Picture Research: Maria Joannou and Ginny Stroud-Lewis
Production: Jonathan Smith

Originated by Dot Gradations Ltd
Printed and bound in China by South China Printing Company

ISBN 1 844 43319 6
08 07 06 05 04
10 9 8 7 6 5 4 3 2 1

British Library Cataloguing in Publication Data
Hibbert, Clare
The Life of a Turtle. – (Life Cycles)
571.8'1792
A full catalogue record for this book is available from the British Library.

Acknowledgements
The publishers would like to thank the following for permission to reproduce photographs:
Ardea pp.**10** (Jean Paul Ferrero), **18** (Adrian Warren), **24** (Ron and Valerie Taylor); Corbis pp. **17** (Lynda Richardson), **21**; FLPA pp.**4** (Minden Pictures), **19** (Gerard Lacz), **20** (Norbert Wu/Minden Pictures), **25** (Gerard Lacz); Imagequest 3-D (V. and W. Brandon) p.**12**; Natural Visions pp.**14**, **15**; Nature Picture Library pp. **28** (Lynn Stone), **29** (Adrian Davies); NHPA pp. **9** (Daryl Balfour), **13** (Anthony Bannister), **16** (Norbert Wu), **22** (Daniel Heuclin), **26** (ANT Photolibrary); Oxford Scientific Films pp.**11** (John L. Pontier), **23** (Howard Hall), **27** (Stan Osolinski); Science Photo Library pp.**5** (Portfield Chickering), **8** (Peter Chadwick).

Cover photograph of a loggerhead turtle, reproduced with permission of FLPA (Minden Pictures).

The publishers would like to thank Janet Stott for her assistance in the preparation of this book.

Every effort has been made to contact copyright holders of any material reproduced in this book. Any omissions will be rectified in subsequent printings if notice is given to the publishers.

The paper used to print this book comes from sustainable resources.

Contents

Any words appearing in bold, **like this**, are explained in the Glossary.

Loggerhead turtles

Sea turtles are **reptiles** that spend most of their lives at sea. Like all reptiles, turtles have a bony **skeleton** and a scaly skin. Turtle babies **hatch** from eggs that are laid on land. They look just like their parents, only much smaller.

This baby loggerhead turtle is hatching from its egg. It has flippers and a shell, just like an adult turtle.

Growing up

Just as you grow bigger year by year, a turtle grows and changes, too. The different stages of the turtle's life make up its **life cycle**. There are several different types of sea turtle, but they all have similar life cycles. This book is about the life cycle of a loggerhead turtle. Loggerheads have big, bony heads.

Where loggerheads live

The place where an animal lives is called its habitat. Loggerhead turtles are found in warm seas, wherever there are plenty of **shellfish**, crabs and sea urchins to eat.

Loggerheads live in warm waters.

A turtle's life

The **life cycle** of a turtle begins when a female comes ashore to lay her eggs. When the eggs **hatch**, the baby turtles scramble down to the sea. The next part of their life is a mystery because they are rarely seen. Young loggerheads hide and feed among the seaweed that floats on ocean **currents**.

After six years or more, the turtles return to the coastlines. Here, they grow even bigger until they are old enough to **mate**. They travel thousands of kilometres back to their nesting grounds, where the females lay their eggs.

Loggerhead life span

Lucky loggerheads live to be 100 years old. Unfortunately, few live that long. Many are eaten by other animals or caught in fishing nets.

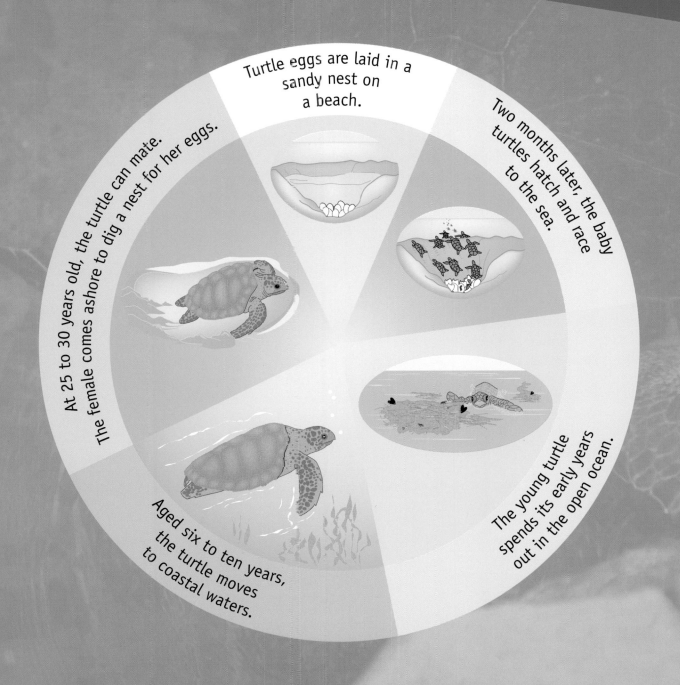

Turtle eggs are laid in a sandy nest on a beach.

Two months later, the baby turtles hatch and race to the sea.

The young turtle spends its early years out in the open ocean.

Aged six to ten years, the turtle moves to coastal waters.

At 25 to 30 years old, the turtle can mate. The female comes ashore to dig a nest for her eggs.

This diagram shows the life cycle of a turtle, from egg to adult.

In the sandpit

Loggerhead turtles dig their nests just above the **high tide line**, where the sea does not reach. This means the eggs will stay dry. The chamber holding the eggs begins about 30 centimetres below the surface of the sand. Inside there are usually about 120 leathery white eggs, each the size of a ping-pong ball.

The female turtle digs her nest on a sandy beach.

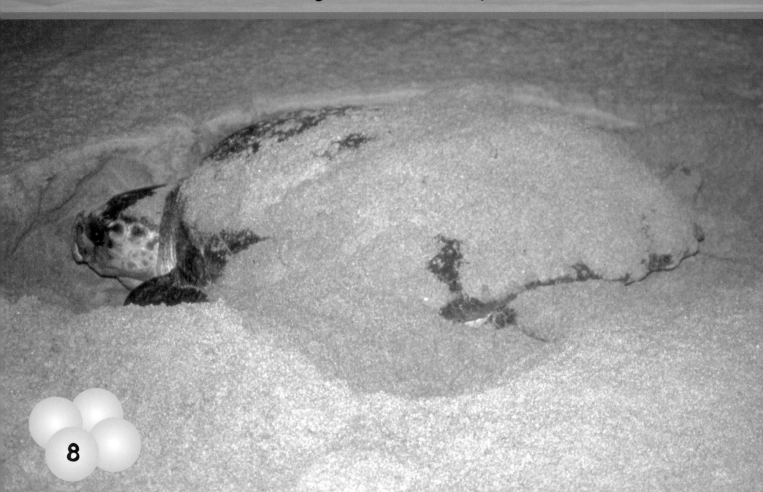

8

Inside the egg

Inside each egg is the beginnings of a turtle, called an **embryo**. For eight to nine weeks, the embryo soaks up the egg's food store, or yolk. It grows from a tiny speck into a miniature turtle. The leathery wall of the egg lets in air, so that the embryo can begin to breathe. Like other **reptiles** that live in the sea, the turtle will need to breathe air for the rest of its life.

The turtle eggs look like leathery ping-pong balls.

Cool boys, hot girls

The **temperature** of the nest is very important. It affects whether the baby turtles will be boys or girls. Low temperatures make male turtles, and high temperatures make females. The turtles lay their eggs in warm **climates** so that there will be plenty of females to lay new eggs in the future.

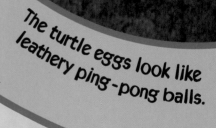

Hatching out

A couple of months after being laid, the eggs **hatch**. Like all baby **reptiles**, loggerheads have a special tooth called the egg tooth. This is sharp enough to cut through the egg's leathery shell, and falls off soon after the turtle hatches.

Nearly there! The hatchling's head and flippers appear first.

Daring diggers

Now the **hatchlings** face a bigger challenge – they are buried alive! Luckily, all the babies in the nest hatch at the same time. They work together, using their flippers as spades. Each hatchling is only about 5 centimetres long, so it can take them a few days to dig through the 30 centimetres or so of sand above them. They will wait for the safety of darkness before breaking through the final centimetres.

Nest-mates reach the surface around the same time.

Nesting season

Most nesting takes place during the summer, when the sun will keep the sand warm. This means that the eggs are ready to hatch in late summer.

Race to safety

Loggerhead parents do not wait near the nest to help their young. **Hatchlings** must find their own way to the shore. They head for the brightest part of the sky – this is a good guide to finding the sea, even at night.

There's no time to lose. **Predators**, or hunters, gather around turtle beaches. The biggest dangers on the beach are crabs and seagulls. In the shallows near the shore, small sharks lie in wait.

The hatchlings race down the beach towards the sea.

Heading towards light

The sea looks bright in the moonlight, but if there are lights from buildings near the beach the hatchlings can be confused. They may head the wrong way and be picked off by predators. On some turtle beaches it is against the law to have lights on at night during nesting season.

Wave goodbye

Using their flippers, the hatchlings flap and crawl down the beach as fast as they can. As the first wave picks them up, the hatchlings swim for the safety of the open sea. Their tiny shells are the perfect shape for slipping through water.

The hatchlings reach the surf. Now they need to catch a wave that will carry them out to sea.

Home on the Waves

The baby turtle is at home in the sea straight away. It can hold its breath only for a short time, so it does not dive far below the surface. It has a good sense of smell, however, and uses this and other tricks to help find its way around. It can even 'read' wave patterns to work out how far from land it is and where food might be.

A turtle's back will blend in with the sea and seaweed. This helps it to hide from overhead predators such as seagulls.

Crafty camouflage

The turtle's colouring helps it to blend in with seaweed when seen from above. Seen from below, the lighter colouring on its belly makes it hard to spot against the bright surface of the sea. This **camouflage** hides the turtle from **predators**. Long flippers help it to cruise through the water, but the turtle can put on a sudden dash of speed if danger threatens.

The turtle's pale underside helps to keep it safe from predators coming from below.

Drinking water

Like every living creature, the young sea turtle needs to drink. There is so much salt in sea water that drinking it would make many animals sick. However, the turtle has a special **gland** that gets rid of the salt.

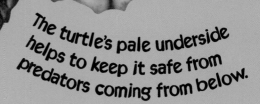

The lost years

There are more **predators** around the coastline, so the young loggerhead turtle stays out in the open ocean while it is growing. This time of its life is sometimes called 'the lost years', because turtle experts often lose track of the young turtles.

The turtle probably spends its lost years among huge floating rafts of seaweed out in the open ocean.

Off track

The turtle travels thousands of kilometres during this time. It drifts along with huge clumps of seaweed, which collect around the edges of big ocean **currents**. Atlantic turtles might drift along the Gulf Stream from the Bahamas all the way over to the Mediterranean Sea. Little is known about what happens to Pacific turtles at this stage.

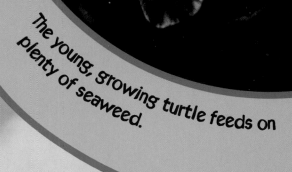

The young, growing turtle feeds on plenty of seaweed.

Family differences

There are two types of loggerhead turtle – one based in the Pacific and Indian Oceans, and one based in the Atlantic Ocean. The most visible difference between them is that the Atlantic loggerhead has two claws on each of its front flippers.

See food, eat food

As the turtle grows, it can hold its breath for longer and dive deeper into the ocean. Its cold blood makes it a better diver than sea **mammals** such as dolphins and killer whales. It can hold its breath for 30 minutes if it wants to chase squid or other **prey**. When it is swimming under water, the turtle closes its nostrils so that no water gets up its nose.

Turtles can eat crabs like this one – shell and all!

Pigging out

The young loggerhead is not a fussy eater. At the surface of the ocean, it munches on seaweed, jellyfish, shrimp, sea snails, fish eggs, tiny plants called **algae**, and any other scraps it can find. Sadly, it sometimes mistakes human rubbish for food. Some turtles die after eating plastic bags, old balloons or foam cups.

The biter bit

Young loggerheads are prey to some of the ocean's biggest **predators** – tiger sharks and killer whales. A loggerhead cannot outswim an attacking shark but, as it grows bigger, it becomes a less attractive meal because of its thick shell.

Killer whales hunt together in groups. As well as sea turtles, their prey also includes fish, seals, penguins and dolphins.

Hard as nails

The young turtle's best defence is the shell around its body. This is made of two parts that grow as the turtle's body grows.

The rings on the turtle's scales tell us how old it is.

Growth rings

You can guess the age of some sea turtles by counting the growth rings on their **scales**. The turtle's scales have to grow at the same rate as its body. Loggerheads are hard to age, however, because the rings quickly become blurry and hard to read.

Bony armour

The strongest part of the shell is the layer of bone beneath the skin. This is the same kind of bone as you have in your spine and ribs. In turtles, these have grown together, or fused, to make a solid suit of armour.

On the turtle's back there is an extra layer of protection made of scales. This is called a carapace. Most loggerheads have ten scales in their carapace. The scales are not made of bone, but of keratin – the same material that makes your fingernails.

The bony armour of this turtle's belly will help to keep it safe.

Teenage turtles

It can take a long time for a loggerhead to grow up. Some stay in the open ocean for over ten years. Others return to coastal waters as young as six years old. They are still not old enough to become parents, but they are now around 50 centimetres long – too big to be bothered by octopuses, small sharks and other **predators**.

As a young adult, the loggerhead moves to shallow waters that are rich in food.

Life in the shallows

In warm, coastal waters there is plenty for the turtle to eat. It roams up and down the coastline, taking advantage of sea **currents** to help it on its way. It hunts along **reefs** and **lagoons**, and even explores the mouths of freshwater rivers. A reef provides shelter for the turtle to rest or hide.

Adult diet

Once it has returned to live near the shore, the turtle can tuck in to its adult diet – crabs, lobsters, sea urchins and **shellfish** such as clams and oysters. The loggerhead's strong jaw allows it to crunch through the shells of its armoured **prey**.

Loggerheads tear into food with their beak-like mouth.

Meeting and mating

A turtle may be 25 to 30 years old before it is ready to **mate**. Then, it leaves its feeding grounds and makes the long journey back to the beach where it was born. This is called **migration**. The turtle's extraordinary journey can be over 10,000 kilometres (6200 miles), and may take one year or more.

Turtle get-together

The loggerheads gather at the nesting grounds in early summer and stay for about two weeks. This is the only time that loggerheads meet up. They spend the rest of their lives alone.

The turtle's journey to its nesting grounds can take longer than a year.

24

Mating

The male attracts the female by touch. He grips her so that she cannot swim off, sometimes leaving claw marks on her shell. He curls his tail around the back of her shell and releases his **sperm**. The female stores the sperm to **fertilize** her eggs with later.

Female turtles often have scratch marks on their shells. These are made by males during mating.

Food shortage

The loggerhead turtles do not feed while they are migrating and mating. They live off stored fat in their bodies. They do not eat again until they return to their feeding grounds.

Back to the beach

After **mating**, male loggerheads return to their feeding grounds. The females are left behind, each with a store of **sperm**. Each female uses some to **fertilize** her first batch of eggs.

One night, the female approaches the beach and crawls on to the sand. It is hard work for a creature that is as heavy as two grown men, but she manages to pull herself along with her flippers. She leaves a wide track behind her.

Female turtles come ashore to lay their eggs.

High and dry

If all is well, she will climb past the **high tide mark** to where the sand is dry and warm, and make her first nest. If the beach seems too busy or noisy, she may turn back to the sea and try again the next night.

The heavy female turtles leave tracks behind them in the sand.

Nifty nesting

Once she has found a good nesting site, the female loggerhead uses her flippers to sweep a big circle in the sand. With her back limbs, she scoops out a hole. She drops a **clutch** of between 50 and 150 eggs into the hole.

Batches of eggs

The female buries the eggs and smoothes the sand to hide her nest. She will come ashore in two weeks' time to lay another clutch. After laying eggs three or four times, she has used up all the stored **sperm** so she returns to her feeding grounds.

The female drops the eggs into the nest one by one.

It may be four years before she is strong enough to cope with another nesting season, but turtles can live as long as 100 years so she has plenty of time. The turtle eggs **hatch** a couple of months after they are laid – and the **life cycle** begins all over again.

Eggs in danger

Before the life cycle can begin again the eggs must survive egg thieves, such as raccoons, opossums and foxes. Although each nest is well-hidden, many are raided.

On this nesting beach, netting and other barriers protect the turtles' nests from humans and animal **predators**.

Find out for yourself

Unless you are lucky enough to live near a turtle beach, it is probably best to find out more by looking on the Internet and reading more books.

Books to read

Lifecycles Migration: The Journey of a Turtle, Carolyn Scarce (Franklin Watts, 2000)

The Life Cycle of a Sea Turtle, Bobbie Kalman (Crabtree Publishing Company, 2002)

Using the Internet

Explore the Internet to find out more about turtles. Websites can change, but if one of the links below no longer works, don't worry. Use a search engine such as www.yahooligans.com, and type in keywords such as 'sea turtle', 'loggerhead', 'hatchling' and 'caretta' (the scientific name for a loggerhead turtle is 'Caretta caretta').

Websites

http://www.turtles.org/kids.htm

A great site with stories and photos about real turtles, plus a webcam.

http://www.cccturtle.org

A wildlife protection website with useful information and pictures of turtles from all over the world.

Disclaimer
All the Internet addresses (URLs) given in this book were valid at the time of going to press. However, due to the dynamic nature of the Internet, some addresses may have changed, or sites may have ceased to exist since publication. While the author and publishers regret any inconvenience this may cause readers, no responsibility for any such changes can be accepted by either the author or the publishers.

Glossary

algae simple, one-celled plants

camouflage colouring or marks on an animal that match its surroundings, making it hard for predators to find them

climate average weather and temperature of a place

clutch group of eggs

current flow of water moving in one direction

embryo baby animal before it has been born or hatched from an egg

fertilize join together male and female parts to create a new living thing

gland special part in a turtle's body that allows it to drink salty sea water without feeling ill

hatch when a young animal comes out of its egg

hatchling young turtle, that has just hatched out of its egg

high tide line highest point on a beach that the tide usually reaches

lagoon small 'sea lake', cut off from the rest of the sea by coral reefs or sand bars

life cycle all the different stages in the life of a living thing, such as an animal or plant

mammal animal that has fur or hair, and that gives birth to its young and feeds them on milk. Seals and humans are mammals.

mate when a male and female animal come together to make eggs or babies

migration regular journey from one habitat to another

predator animal that hunts other animals and eats them for food

prey animal that is hunted by other animals for food

reef underwater structure, built up from sand, rocks or the skeletons of millions of tiny creatures, called corals

reptile cold-blooded animal that has a bony skeleton and scaly skin. Turtles, snakes, lizards and crocodiles are all types of reptile.

scale one of the horny plates on a turtle's shell

shellfish sea creatures that have a stony shell that protects their soft, boneless bodies

skeleton bones that make up an animal's body

sperm male sex cells

temperature how hot or cold something is

Index

Titles in the *Life Cycles* series include:

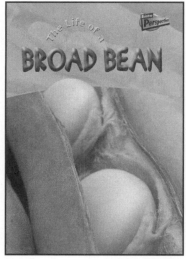

Hardback   1 844 43314 5

Hardback   1 844 43315 3

Hardback   1 844 43317 X

Hardback   1 844 43316 1

Hardback   1 844 43318 8

Hardback   1 844 43319 6

Find out about the other titles in this series on our website www.raintreepublishers.co.uk